Wheelings

Wheelings

Doris Hillis

Thistledown Press Ltd.

Canadian Cataloguing in Publication Data

Hillis, Doris, 1929-

Wheelings

Poems.

ISBN 1-895449-37-5

I. Title.

PS8565.I484W4 1995   C811'.54   C95-920163-7
PR9199.3.H548W4 1995

Book design by A.M. Forrie
Cover art by K.Gwen Frank
Set in New Baskerville
by Thistledown Press Ltd.

Printed and bound in Canada
by Hignell Printing
Winnipeg, Manitoba

Thistledown Press Ltd.
633 Main Street
Saskatoon, Saskatchewan
S7H 0J8

Acknowledgements

Many of these poems have appeared or are forthcoming in the following
magazines: *Reflections, The Burning Bush, Briarpatch,
Germination, Borealis, The Prairie Journal of Canadian Literature,
Western People, Our Family, Other Voices, FreeFall*; and in the anthologies:
Alberta Poetry Yearbook (1979); *Dancing Visions* (Thistledown, 1985);
Beyond Bad Times (Snowapple Press, 1993); and some have been broadcast
on CBC Radio's "Ambience".

The author would like to thank Paddy O'Rourke
for his editorial assistance.

This book has been published with the assistance of The Canada Council
and the Saskatchewan Arts Board.

For Bill, Sandy and Tyler

CONTENTS

We shall not cease from exploration
and the end of our exploring
will be to arrive where we started
and know the place for the first time.

— John Fowles

Everything speaks of the Great Spirit.
It is here all around us; it is here deep inside us.
There is nothing that isn't in its essence Spirit.

The Great Spirit moves in the mighty oceans,
in the serene mountains, in earth's diversity.
It is there in the order of spheres and stars,
the ever-changing moon.

> Open our eyes, O Spirit, that we may see.
> Open our ears, that we may hear.
> Sharpen our senses, O Great Spirit,
> that we may know and feel your presence.

The Great Spirit sings in our swirling rivers,
our dancing winds.   It is folded within
the smallest seed and unfurls in the simplest blossom.

It is there in the merriment of our children;
and in our kinsfolk — the creatures of the earth.
It is in their voices, their cries, their songs . . .
and in their silences.

> Open our eyes, O Spirit, that we may see.
> Open our ears, that we may hear.
> Sharpen our senses, O Great Spirit,
> that we may know and feel your presence.

Eternally
questing mind
teases time
for timeless totality
worries ceaselessly for wholeness
craving the One

(Pueblo Indian Legend)

Spider Grandmother sat pondering. She was thinking of beginning; she was thinking of increase; she was thinking of naming.

She spoke a word and the night came into being — deep night, black night, night of her first spinning.

Then from her own substance she spun a bright jewel, the Sun; from her own substance she spun yet another, the Moon.

With a flick of her long fingers she wove a tapestry of stars. With a flick of her long fingers she wove the Milky Way, and within it, an orb of exquisite beauty, the Earth.

Then out of her ponderings she wove a web that embraced everything; a web so fine it could never be seen; a web so strong it could never be broken; a web so all-encompassing that nothing existed without its presence.

And within this sacred web was woven the Fate of Humankind, drawn from her long-fingered memory, and having no end.

Come   *creeping people,* dance in the ring:
     Coppergold viper chevroned with black
     Quick-shinnying chameleon of varying hues
     blind tunnelling earthworm tuned to a tremble

Come   *flying people,* dance in the ring:
     Waddle-rolly puffin, beak rainbowed like a clown
     Blackcapped tern, world-traveller, with sickle-arched
     wings
     Blue gauzy dragonfly and pug-faced bat

Come   *swimming people,* dance in the ring:
     With a flip of your tail, great whale, twist and cavort
     Dart o shoal of herring, slivers of silver moon
     Float and sway, crystal jelly, venomous Man-of-War

Come   *standing people,* dance in the ring:
     Old Mother Silvertip with lumbering gait
     Sleek spotted cheetah, sinuous and fleet

     And Monkeykind

     And Humankind

     Hand and paw, fist and claw

     All Nature's children, children of the Earth
     Come dance, dance together, in the ring of Life

Springcrisp morning
sunshine from a scoured sky —
and between cedar bough and spruce
is spooled the delicate orb of the spider
the silver argiope
A web of life and death
its tensile rays and spirals
are patterned by an inner law
and deftly woven from the common substance
of the Living Void
the stuff of burned-out stars
This subtle gossamer taut resilient
in its equipoise and momentary perfection
is a holy diadem

a slender goddess
comes softly swinging
in her chariot of gold and lavender

She is drawn by cats plush subtle
One is tortoise-shell multihued as the colours of life
one is black/white stark as paradox
Eyes flash tails lash
Restively they tongue their silver bits.

She is dressed in white hawk's plumage
closely moulded to her small round breasts
and at her throat the glittering Brisinga-men
She bends from her chariot anointing the earth
with tears and when she smiles
melting streams swirl in frothy eddies
dazzle like rainbow

Everywhere   crisp growth
juice alive in root and stem
the putting on of rain-sweet mantles
Everywhere spring's urgency
bursts the woody strangles
of a past season

A tilt of April sunshine
Cottonwhite puffs travel the blue blue sky
Still a nip in the air
when rosy-cheeked kids
(elfcurls peeking from caps and toques)
slither atop the rotting snowdunes
and jump . . . their small arms
whirling like rotors
Little dudes
treadle a shard of broken picket
over the knobbly stones
in gooey black gummy
Fun! Fun! stamping sloshing
squealing with joy . . .
splattering the lovely licorice ooze
. . . all over

At last at last it's Spring!

April
in England
a morning after rain
and the sluiced sun
dances

Bare toes
in the wet
warm grass
test the earth's
quickening

Soon
comes the season
of planting

That first warm day
the children race from schoolyard
to riverside park
peeling off jackets mittens scarfs
Youngsters in bright shirts and blouses
their jean-pockets weighted
with the frosties rainbows
blood-alleys and snakies
they treasure
Clusters of watchers
come down the ice-rutted paths
to goad on the rivals:
Petra Robert Philip Beth
as they pit their skills
The contestants kneel
in silky dust
arms flexed fingers poised
Shoot the slick marbles
from grass tuft to grass tuft
down scarps gullies fissures crannies
across miniature eskers
Their small mouths pursed
they squint the angle
measure the shot
target the artful winner

She is a miracle of new life   May-born
lovely slender filly fine as a gazelle
She runs close to the mare's shoulder
not even a sliver of light
cuts between them
She canters over the green turf
shies at her own shadow
One minute   timid   fey
she peeks
then smart as whipcrack
polkas away
A pert coquette
she tosses her flirt
of forelock   her tasselled tail
flags high
pivots on tall quarters
trots like quicksilver

This dainty arabian
speaks the zenith of endless suns
is felicity   certitude   benediction

Buzz of winglets
Flash of burnished copper
A hummingbird at the fuchsia bloom
hangs suspended
probing deeply the blossom's scarlet throat
I watch this febrile acrobat
sip his fill
and dart from flower to flower
twirling in his wake
yellow grains
that touch
quicken

Today I hear the lilt of waltzes
Lehar   Waldteufel   Strauss
and I think of those zestful
years when I was five
the boisterous wireless booming

I see you dancing   miming to the music
opening windows on sunny mornings
letting in the trill of song-thrush
from the rosebower   cheep of bluetit
chaffinch   all the summer humming
sounds carried on the breeze

You trip   twirl   sing   whistle
in your honeyed world
as you flick the furniture
with feather-duster scattering motes
till the redwood tables gleam
You whisk around vases
sprigged with fresh flowers

Then you take me in your arms
your last child   your third
my curled hands clinging tight
and wing me easy   wing me high
in your swirling

She was always close
to cool my childhood fevers
and her songs at bedtime lullabied
the phantoms away

From her I learned earth's lore
lessons of swinging tides
ways of gliding birds
At the drawling out of evening
she read for me
sky's deep crimsons and violets

I recall her hands
working the soil   pressing in
springtime's secret bulbs
culling summer's blossoms
and the talisman she once placed
in my open palm: polished seed
of chestnut dark and smooth
smelling of root and saplings greening

You remember the rainy nights
of childhood: the storm's first
wild explosion trouncing the house
stropping grey windows   fat beads
of water sperming down
                    . . . and the capricious
rhythm of squalls hitting the walls
in splats   like grain
thrown against plywood
or the heavy drum of hands

How you nestled
in your bed beneath crisp sheets
and hugged your teddy bear
its worn body loved and laundered
to plushness white threads
There you hoarded your comfort
wrapping it round you tightly —
listening to quiet voices
below stairs   the shift of fire tongs
and logs

All night
        you drifted in and out of sleep
to the steady lullaby
until the whisperings dwindled
and the single measured drops
pearled themslves
to silence

Ride him! Ride him pardner!
My mother's laughter as she lifts high
the old black broomstick with the stallion's head
she's made me: its paper-bag jowels
flared nostrils crayoned in
whited eyes   curling lips
The long thin loop of leather

Ride him! she calls *Ride him child!*
Tame him   Make him your own
I swing astride his back
cavort   hold his head tall
ginger him with a rowan whip
against my thigh

Away down the narrow path I prance
through the jostle of bushes
shying   pawing
careening this way and that

I sit his feisty bucks   his wild rearings
Thunder him madly (myself worn breathless) . . .
then canter   whinnying
back to the open lawn
where mother stands waiting

As I gentle him   whoa him
to a halt
her eyes burn bright

As I reached my twenties
(with a shrug of the shoulders
and excitement in my heart)
I set out to seek new latitudes

The mother I left
has lived more than half a lifetime
without me
She has grown old wearied
by the years
I grieve never being with her
never being there to ease the tedium
of her shut-in days
On every visit when we part
I see in her eyes
that clubbed-down look

And now my daughter
has reached her twenties
full of the zing and sass of youth
her temper like tinder
brimming with wild dreams
and brash impatience
She spurns my middle age fears
and with a shrug of the shoulders
answers the siren call

This crisp May morning shimmers
                              like Chablis
Cliff escarpments dazzle white
before a kneeling blue sea
and the sun burns bright
across my face

Quick! Quick! a flicker of feathers
the quiffed crest . . .
a small spry bird
jockeys soft bunts of wind
riding up   up   up
above the rolling hills
                          the patchwork fields
fluttering   floating
dancing lightly
in high ether

till the singer   beyond sight
becomes a disembodied voice
sublime   free
spilling back to earth its twitter-lilt
the liquid loveliness   the promise
of its song

Storm warnings all day . . .
The springtide racing
driven by furious westerlies

You and I in our borrowed oilskins
sou'westers   boots
dash down the cobbled stepways
to the harbour to see the whitecaps barrelling in
breaking   spuming
across the tall sea-wall
We link our arms for safety
beat crabwise into the massive brunt of wind
angling from right to left   left to right
along the granite causeway
With every tack we flex our heads
to catch breath   the blast snatching
our words   our laughter
Tousled   drenched with spray
we battle the sea's tantrums
and gaze into the vortex
of foam   just a single
railing   so close to the edge . . .
And then we turn back to the hillside town
hurry through darkened lanes
to a secluded bar   snug behind
thick oak doors   descend
steep stairs to dusky warmth
the smell of smoke and liquor

We sip a glass of cognac savour a turkish cigarette
You have my absolute attention and I have yours
our eyes meeting levelling holding . . .
And I know
you will always be part of me
no matter how our lives may change
or distances divide

I remember how you read the weathers of my mind

They were the green years   the nights we sat by moonlight
on the cliff's crag   listening to the gentle sough
of wind among pines   watching the floodtide lather
granite anvils

Your presence and the white moon's sorcery
wakened me for always
to the allurement of shimmering seas   distant stars

Hearts at ease   we talked of childhood days
opened our worlds to each other   our privacies
weaving a covenant of trust

Just friends
yet in the eloquence of silence . . .
closer than lovers

Your presence was the hub
of my being As long as you were there
I knew my place   my home   my centre

In your last years
you gathered yourself ever inward
allowing your body to speak
its own punctual death

We talked often of life's
fleeting until there was nothing more
to say   just our hands joined
sharing silence

And then you grew far-distant
beyond my reaching:
a nomad soul never quailing
from your lone journey

With your parting
I am matriarch in your stead
awaiting the wheelings of time

Maybe this was what she was searching for
at thirty   Redirection for her life
Far away from urban rat-race
the dryness   rigidity of academia
A place sheltered
by his caring   commitment
joy that grew with marriage
the wished-for child
the sharing
Here prairie storms broke against
stalwart backs of trees and gentled flakes
drifted into her garden
bringing needed moisture
for rerooting   for her returning spring
Here was a sanctum
where she could ponder civilities of living
   . . . the measures . . .
allowing calm weathers to compose her thoughts
In this afternoon of quiet years
she found the gift
to speak exultantly
in her own voice

How he's changed you   this child
conjured from your body
His being has given you reason
to look within   to free your own person:
that shy spirit once whelmed
by utter loneliness

His sweetness and dependency
have opened floodgates
letting your love flow
like strong rivers

Now you are committed —
know pride   patience
the generosity of wide horizons
He is your boon companion
has made your days
holy again
has made you whole woman

Your two-year old grandson
goes with you everywhere
He's playing in the flowerbed
opening mouths of snapdragons
stroking their plush lips
He picks the pansy-faces
pressing orange and black velours
close to his cheek
sniffs the spiced ruff of marigold
Then he's away to your workshop
drawn by the mystery
of spindle and wheel
Tiny hands toy with your booty of gadgets
nuts and bolts that fit and thread
couplers and sockets
His dark eyes widen in droll expressions
each breathtaking moment
When you call him to come
he throws you that mischievous
grin of contrariness
that says: he just isn't ready
just hasn't time
has this whole fresh world to explore
don't you know!

At last the longed-for day
and a little boy rides on a fireman's shoulders
his heart thrilling to the "All aboard!
All aboard for the Disneyland train!"

Afar from hospitals and doctors he lives
these moments of remission
He sways above the jubilant
holiday crowds jazzy in their tee-shirts
and shades: fathers cuddling babes
in snugglies   mothers trailing nutbrown
children by the hand

And Byron feels so kingly
a Goofy cap perched on his rosinsmooth head
the hippity-flippity ears awagging
as the fireman sashays below him
down Main Street U.S.A.
The music plays and the Disneyland
family parades and buffoons: Pluto and Mickey
Donald and Minnie   The Big Bad Wolf
Three Little Pigs   all swaying   bowing
waltzing the children

He rides high and merry through all
the wondrous Kingdoms
through Sleeping Beauty's castle   the snowdraped Matterhorn
until the bright sun burns low
from a blueberry sky and the drowsy child
coves gently in his fireman's arms

I look at you across the table
your face tooled by the years

I recall another place another time:
a tall villa above the pastel town
its garden skipping down
to the azure sea
a sun-room of cyclamen
and beyond east windows
mimosas in bloom

Our days together were madcap dreams
of countries we would travel
And we did

Here we meet again
older now   wiser
rich with other loves
and children

You hold in your hand a fruiting dandelion
its golden head now grey   delicate   symmetrical
a perfect globe   its button-scalp
a launching pad for each beaked and feathery seed
You play a child's game   blow   blow   blow again
telling the hours   till all have flown away

You think of your children   their growing years
their turning outward
How soon the time is ripe and you must ready
them for the wind's embrace

I sense her watching

Eyes molten in moonshine   she lies
along the bough of a silver fir
Dark spotted cat   knowing
the sweet ache of my hunger
uncoils her sinuous body
singing like a lover

I run my fingers round her neck
and stroke the crown of her questing head

From her eyes dart starfires
that electrify my body
and excite my lips to song

        And when she steals away
imprinted on my vibrant flesh —
stigmata of claws

Under blind of night
black stallion   steelgrey mares
jostle and chafe
until the circling drove
breaks
Hurricane horses   red eyes bared
stream   silver   pewter
across the sky
Slash of ironshod hoof
strikes flame   Forked light
leaps high
They wheel in their rage
heads upflung   manes
sheeting back   mouths
lathered white

He carried the grey cat
like an offering
His daughter touched the limp form
Her blind fingers followed evasion's edge
shaping the adult lie

They took her
      to the sockeye spawning stream
in the last cold days of Fall
      where the clear waters
were a crimson seethe of fish
      She watched

the fevered writhings
      of females swollen with eggs
and the twistings of males
      their nuptial jaws
snapping like pit-bulls
      to survive   to breed

while along dense riverbanks
      among coiling roots of trees
and trailing weed
      the putrid flesh from previous days
lay snagged   bleached   bloated
      And the image

of this common death
      this cyclic certainty
predestined macabre
      incised her mind
for ever   deep
      as a torture burn

LAMENT OF THE FEEDER CALVES

(From within the only grassless lot they know)

All we do is
       eat and shit/eat and shit/eat and shit/eat and shit
       eat and shit/eat and shit/eat and shit/eat and shit
       eat and shit/eat and shit/eat and shit/eat and shit
until the day of
       the electric prod/one-way chute/cattleliner/slaughter

Every week the mothers of grief
gather in the Plaza de Mayo
They wear white kerchiefs
that bear the names of lost children
Their eyes scan the faces of strangers
ever searching for a loved one

The Mothers of the Plaza de Mayo
have carried children in their wombs
flesh of their flesh
They have asked the Junta:
Where are our children?
and been given lies
they have been beguiled
by zealots with fastidious hands
who lease out secret butcheries

Their tears turn to vitriol
despair to wills of steel
Their witness cries out
Libertad! Libertad!

They drop by singly or in pairs
the small-town has-beens of coffee-row

They off-set the tedium of their days
with blather   beefs   bullshit
and recount endless anecdotes
of tough drought-stricken years

Fumbling tri-focals   wiping rheumy eyes
they dither
over health and wealth
while their children
powered by muscle and purpose
and ideas spawned of book and campus
usurp their place

A woman sits slumped
against a concrete slab on a concrete floor
at the end of a walkway of cells

She stares through barred windows
towards the world   beyond
key   lock   fences of barbed wire

She rolls another cigarette
smoothes it   touches it gently
to her lips   to the lighted match
and sucks in deeply
to quell the waves
of nausea

A woman watches rectangles of sunlight
on the floor   hard-edged
by shadow
Lies down   letting the dark grill
fetter her flesh

Slowly she unclenches

THE PRICE
Indian Territory by Edward Poitras

On the hard gallery floor
seven sculptured Indian figures
are knuckled double
Foreheads pressed to ground
they are faceless
Their lacerated scalps are hanked
with horsehair from the abattoir
Their trussed-back arms
lashed tightly at the wrists
are shackled from above
by ropes

We had agreed: *No more*

I'm pregnant   you announce
your eyes unleashing fire

It has happened insidiously
this new one budding
in your womb

Your children   the family
you brought me ready-made
eat up our daily space
like cowbird chicks

You stress again: *No more you understand!*

I take you to the clinic
While we wait: *Do you wish
to change your mind?*   I ask
I could urge: Let's have
just this child

Yet my tongue sulks silent

I kiss you softly as you leave
drive down city streets
wringing the steering wheel

You strove hard to offer your love
to forge strong bonds
in his early childhood years
And now —
this deep estrangement

You have lost him to punk peers
porn video   the arcade underworld
He has run full gamut:
lies   school-suspensions   petty theft

He knows his style
offends you: tight levis
black leathers   studded
He smirks into your face
when you confront him

He is caught up in a world
of slick piranhas
          And you dread each day

I examine the sunflower that flourishes
each season   Blooms   seeds   grows fragile —
brittle fragments speaking its identity

Autumn frailings in the dust

My face in reflection
bears resemblances of you
flesh falling into folds   shadows
worry-lines   creases at eye and lip . . .
your likeness in my walk   my stoop   my gesture

I'm ninety-eight
When I was born Queen Victoria
was on the throne of England
How can I tell you what it's like
to be old?

I have watched my body age:
arms grow pretzel
frail and skin turn toady
nails coarsen to yellow claws

My eyes are bleared
I cannot see the print of books
details of photographs
I am always beyond earshot
beyond the elusive shape of words
My legs have stiffened to brittle sticks
As I walk I tremble   clench
the arms of nurses
I am led   lifted   sponged   changed   fed
dressed like a doll   and left

If people come I spell
the contours of their faces with my fingertips
Sometimes I know them
and sometimes lose them in the
mazes of my mind   and then
nothing matters any more
Nothing and nobody

At this time you only want the nostalgia
of yesterday   reaching back
to past years   to good health
before the trauma . . . realizing
some things can never be made well
          ever again

You are pared down
to skin and bone   And drugs
that hold the pain at bay
leave you torpored   ashen

I cradle you in my arms
rocking you   watching
 your slow dying

    Armfuls of syringa
          brim a tall ceramic vase
efflorescence of snow on a cherry wood table
frail white blossoms against the deepening dark

From my window I see clear azure
widening between black clouds
                unfolding outwards
At last
   a fine sky at eventide
lightening the shadowy corners
Soon I'll have honeysuckle at my threshold
sweet grapes heavy on the vine

    And the sky
          this burning sky
brightens the horizon to flame   flushes the cherry wood
to ruby   the white syringa
          the silvering dusk

After the war
my father grew roses   climbing roses
he twined on trellises
weaving supple arms through rustic lattice —
his bower a sanctuary

He was a man
driven to make amends for deeds
forced on him —
tending roses he said
because my mother prized
their lustrous flounces

But he really grew them for himself
to ease disquietude
by nurturing something beautiful
with caring hands

On summer evenings
they would go together to the fragrant arbour
he with secateurs   she
bearing a cloth of folded damask
and one by one he culled
the long stemmed flowers
laying them lovingly
in the cradle of her arm

September by the lake   a house
on a hillside quilled

with pines   Wood warblers sing
almost to the dying days

of Fall   and roses
furl back their petals

in final adoration
to a mellow sun

This landscape
has paths to stroll   trees

to lie under   windsong   beesong
lapping water

Here I quell my fears
wind down   wind down

let past years rest
and the future be

Here you come at evening
when meltflow rises to peaks of foam
and the fragile mayflies hover
and dance in warm sunlight
You step from stone to stone
waiting with easy stance
as the live stream lullabies around you

These are the moments of promise
when you flex your arm and shoulder
in measured swing   so deftly
The rod is your mystic wand
and you cast the parabola of line
as far upstream as you can reach
cutting the shiny surface
watching the curved lash   the delicate lure
glide back
       down   down   towards you

Now you fish for rainbows
                one by one
playing beguiling conjuring
their secrets
as they dance   thrash   leap
stand tall on supple tails
in a radience of blue   of silver

For those brief moments
they hold you
before you set them free
return them to the timeless currents

Hedged roads twist
through rolling countryside
Slate roofed cottages nestle close to the village church
their summer gardens blazing bright
with lupins   larkspur
And beyond elm coppices
stretch the playingfields   the manicured gardens
of the College   the Monastery of Kelham

A house once built for lords and ladies
and their pleasures
this residence with its domed chapel
is now an oasis of peace
a place of prayer and the parley of minds

On windy days monks in girdled cassocks
spinnaker from House   from College
Black robes swish over polished floors
as they enter the sanctuary

Here they learn the amplitude of faith
Young men ponder the purpose of their being
and grey-haired patriarchs
who have borne Christ's yoke a lifetime
exult in the ripeness of His Love

TO THE GLORY OF GOD IN HIS WILL
— *The Kelham Christus*

Bells call for prayers
Monks novices postulants
lcave their quarters
and file through the cloisters
to the sanctuary

This brotherhood of silent men
bonded by their covenant with Christ
bow their heads in worship
genuflect before the altar
intone the daily liturgy

Their Christus on the Cross
is a virile God-man
crowned with thorns
His rivetting eyes drill deeply
to their souls' root

She survives just one day at a time
her widowed world compressed
within parentheses of walls

Memories ago
her house bustled youngsters
laughter   hopes   dreams

Gone   Gone   children to distant cities
old friends dead

Her cat is everything
She loves him fiercely as she's never loved

Cosied close beside her night or day
his presence brings repose

The amber prairie unrolls
its sweeping canvas to the horizon's rim
Sounds of lowing cattle
resonate in the pristine chill

The fields are fruiting   They smell of sun-warmed grain
Bearded heads of barley bow low
Wheat swaths girdle and golden
the rounded hills
A mirror of prussian blue   the slough still
in its nest of shrub and reed
Along damp margins shore birds
spear for food and run   run
spelling the neat calligraphy
of their passing

High above wild turkeys float in azure sky
their burblings buoying the polished air

At first a solitary one or two
flutter on the southward wind
dipping to alight and cling
to eucalyptus leaves
And then others   hundreds   thousands
follow the pattern of their innate maps
drifting in on saffron gauze
fragile   tremulous

With the turning season
butterflies pilgrim against the storms
over forests plains and mountains
to ancestral grounds
and settling to rest they close their wings

There is a place
I visit   A pool
shined by sunlight
where the blue heron comes
at evening
He stands at the water's edge
elegant   poised
a seeker
And I
his acolyte

November days   the land is silent
and the chill sooty-smelling air
is mingled with woodsmoke

The earth gives her body
to the jovial sun
The dog is twinned by his long shadow
Complacent cats wash their faces
twice over

As I walk among spruces
and apple trees their arms raised
like prophets
my tensions slip away
and I exult

First light coverings of snow
quilt the prairie   Enough to saddle
the forks of trees   whiten window ledges
Then a melding of weathers   moist ice-fog
rolls in   thick like wadding

The morning after
bright sun breaks through   loosening
dissapating . . .
Magically a new sky widens
overhead
Shadows purple the snow
Spare shrubs are fringed with hoar
their black bones sharp as graphics
The house stands tall   its angularities
etched in winter flame   picture book clear
Farm buildings rimed
blaze their damp prime colours
The air is taffeta-crisp

This hushed landscape
sheathed   ruffed
smooth ermine lawns untrodden

everywhere . . . flowerings

        of frost

Prairie   wide
          as the latitudes of prayer
so silent I hear
          my heart's measured pulse
No birds   no shadows under the oyster clouds
My nostrils fill with frost's cold
          fragrance
as I walk the snow-fringed paths
          shoeing soft flakes aside

I am empty of memories
          and the pressures of the morrow
am held in this rare stasis
My eyes are lost to an infinite
          horizon
the oneness   earth and sky

At our lakeside cottage   huge flakes
giddy down in gusts
swaying tall evergreens   fidgetting the last
frail ash-key from its rigid branch
Our eaves are heavy with drift
the fencepost sculptured in furls

We draw near to the crackling fire
watch dancing shadows on rough log walls

Our passions have mellowed now
We are content
to live with opacities
Our bodies nestled
against the frosty chill
we find together   plenitude   tenderness
fidelity we can rest in

Shrubs   snowcapped
Pathways   muffled

Frost ferns on the windows
A filigree of silence   hands folded